God's Book
1

Protagonist Press

God's Book 1
First Printing
Copyright ♥ 2017
Protagonist Press
TheSynthesisFoundation.org

All rights reserved.
No part of this book may be reproduced, stored in a retrieval system, or transmitted in any form or by any means, electronic, mechanical, photocopying, recording or otherwise, without the prior written permission of the author.

Printed in the United States of America

ISBN: 978-1-941587-03-4

Dedicated to Govinda,
the Lord of lords, King of kings, God of gods
and Father of all living beings
and to His lady and beloved, Radha.

TABLE OF CONTENTS

Editor's Preface	1
Introduction	3
The Journey of Consciousness	6
God is Your Love	8
The Blessing of a Genuine Teacher	11
In the Footsteps of the Masters	14
The Name	17
Your Real Self	21
Spiritual Practice	26
Finding the Beloved in All	30
Devotional Service	33
The Awakening of Divine Love	37
Remember	42
Poetry	45

Editor's Preface

God's Book 1 is drawn from a series of meditations that were given by God through a human instrument. These writings hold much inspiration and truth and often reference many of the world's great sages and teachers - Jesus Christ, Krishna, Yogananda, Ramakrishna, Meher Baba and more. As these writings are a compilation of transcribed meditations, we beg the reader's indulgence if a direct quotation is not provided. We are indebted to these great souls for their eternal words of wisdom and for pointing the way.

Though there are many ways to refer to the Divine, this has been written in the masculine form, God. If one prefers the feminine form, Goddess, or any other preferred forms, feel free to read the passages accordingly. The teachings are universal and are here for all religions and philosophies.

We hope you enjoy this compendium and take deeply to heart the echo of the Divine that this lovely book provides.

Introduction

*I am here to speak to you about the one great truth
which is in every religion of the world;
the truth that is the underlying Divine Ground
of every path…and that is Love.*

Blessed one, this book is a spiritual blueprint to an awakened consciousness of God. It is a roadmap outlining the basic principles of every religion to assist you in fulfilling your quest for spiritual awakening. Contained within these writings are the sacred teachings of grace that have bridged the east and the west with the living light of Love. This book is not intellectual; it is designed to awaken and open your heart so you can experience the genuine happiness and fulfillment you are seeking.

May you take this as spiritual food for your soul in the same way that you take in physical food for your body. The love and spirit of the Blessed One within everyone is the food that is within these words. So do not let your heart and soul go hungry, for as Christ said, *"Man does not live by bread alone, but by every word that comes out of the mouth of God."* (Matthew 4:4)

Remember that behind these words and every letter written here is the Sweet One. Behind all apparent separation and differences is the Blessed One who loves you and is the open secret... I invite you to please slow down now, open your heart and take in deeply the underlying truth within and behind these sacred and direct messages to you. There is nothing more important than your heart feeling a love that lasts.

Namaste

I bow to the God that dwells within you,
all around you,
above you, below you
and inside you,
as you.

He dwells within your consciousness
as your consciousness
awakens.

God is your consciousness reading this.

Let go and let God awaken your consciousness.
Give your consciousness to Him
in this very moment,
here and now.

The Journey of Consciousness

*The Eternal Truth
is the Consciousness of ever new and endless Bliss,
which is right here with you and in you,
one with you, and as you.*

I am here to serve as a tour guide on the journey of consciousness which is common to all true paths. On this journey you can see that consciousness is the common factor in all existence; the existence you are now perceiving is consciousness.

Consciousness is "the commons" of the universe. Your consciousness and all consciousness is God's consciousness. You do not have consciousness, you *are* consciousness. God does not have consciousness, He *is* consciousness. He is your consciousness, and He is you. You are His consciousness—all this is God's consciousness...and this consciousness is the Divine Ground of all existence.

The Divine Ground is omnipresent, which means that it is right here where you are now, whether you can see it or not. The teacher's task is to reveal to you this indwelling Presence, which is the presence of God's Consciousness residing in your consciousness here and now. Awaken!

This journey of consciousness leads to the center of your heart, the core of your being. The center of your heart is Love Divine, the Living Spirit. This same Living Spirit is talking to you through these words, and this Living Spirit is you in essence, in that you are a part of It. It is your Self. Know that the journey need not take an entire lifetime, for this center is immanent, right here in your love for one another.

To the degree you love, to that precise degree you journey deeper into the center of your soul where God dwells. It is by degrees of love that you sail into the center until you finally reach the deepest part of your real Self, which is God and His bliss. This center is where God dwells, and He is right here now.

By giving Him your full attention and taking this message to heart, your heart is opening to God, who is the deeper part of your Self. This is a choice on your part, for you always have the freedom to choose. And when you choose Him, you are choosing to believe in the good, in God, in Love Supreme.

God is Your Love

*God is the love you share with your your family,
your friends, and all others.*

We live in a period that seeks world peace more than ever before, yet the peace we seek will never come through political ideology or mere religion. The only answer is through humanity knowing love — a real and definite love as that felt by a parent for their children. When this love is understood at its essence, one realizes that it is the same unconditional love that God feels for His children also. God loves you in the same way you love your children, only it is divinely amplified and unconditional. This love ends all fear and separation between people. Every parent has within them the same love for their children as God has for His.

Contemplate how your love for your children is a reflection of God's love for all His children everywhere. God loves you and everyone in the same way that you love your children, only more. It is this love from God that is helping you now, just as every breath you breathe is a gift to you from Him.

What is causing the selfish consciousness in the world? The problem is that humankind is ignoring God. Even though humanity walks around in His presence, they are ignoring Him and cannot see Him because their behavior has lowered their sensitivity to Him. Man's consciousness must be raised into the understanding of Love. Mere religion will not do it. Only love will save humanity. Through working with a genuine teacher, one can learn how Divine Love (which is within you and everyone) will overcome all fear, doubt, anger and hatred.
This awakening of love will render humanity whole, and they will once again realize the great love that their divine parent God has for them.

Feeling loved, humanity will have hope. Having hope, they will develop faith, and through faith they will have the persistence in their search to apply daily, loving, gradual lifestyle changes. This will open their hearts and allow the Divine Love of God to radiate out into the world, bringing a world peace that is transformative and lasting. This awakening is being transmitted to you now through these writings.

The goal then is to love your family, friends, and others more and more. You do not have to always love what they do, but love the soul that dwells within them and remember to give the charity of forgiveness. God will then give you the gift of Divine Love which is now awakening inside the secret garden of your heart as you read this... gently, quietly. Let it awaken in you.

Contemplate for a moment that the love you feel for one another is God. God is love, so God is the love you feel for one another. Only God as love is ultimately the real, underlying Reality of this existence, the Divine Ground of this material ground. Love is the innermost self in every person, including you. So let us take in deeply the words Lord Krishna says at the end of the sacred text, *The Bhagavad Gita*, which confirms the beauty and the wonderful truth that your love is God:

> *"To love is to know Me,*
> *My innermost nature,*
> *The Truth that I Am."*
> (B.G. 18:55)

Through this knowledge, you enter at once to the Divine Being. This happens every time you love. This is the real path, the path of love, the path of God, for God is love. God is all in all.

The Blessing of a Genuine Teacher

May we all remember that knowing God should be our number one priority.

There is an old story in India that relates how long ago a spiritual amnesia spread across the world where people forgot their union with God, with Love. It spread further, and people forgot that they wanted God. Some people even forgot that they had a heart and that love was the key to their real happiness. So they began to look for it in other objects and places rather than in their hearts, until one day a loving teacher showed up and reminded them of the truth.

He shared the timeless truth that only knowing your heart will make you happy and only the deep soul-love of God can reach deep enough into your heart to bring lasting happiness.

Once that was understood, the people were willing to work hard for that lasting happiness again by making a gentle but daily effort to attain it. They followed through on the guidance given by the teacher and once again felt God and His love in their hearts, giving them the lasting happiness that they had always been seeking.

Buddha said that life has much suffering in it. When you understand this then you are ready for the first great teaching: In every age, God arranges a way for souls to overcome suffering and find lasting happiness with the help of a genuine teacher or guide of s*at* (divine truth). A s*at* guide or teacher is one who teaches just to love quietly and gently more and more... a little bit each day... for that is the way of love, and God is love.

The first thing that our egos must accept is that one cannot do this by oneself. All great realized beings such as Christ, Krishna, Buddha and Rama espoused this truth, and they themselves sought and found a living teacher, who is simply a master of himself. To call someone a master can be profoundly misunderstood, for in truth we are only masters of ourselves.

We must find a living teacher of divine truth and befriend them, ask for their guidance and be receptive to their instructions. We then allow them to become our teacher. The entire purpose of the spiritual path is to evolve from unconsciousness to consciousness, from lack of heart to heartfelt, through the blessing of a s*at* teacher.

The goal is to live in humble, loving service to all, remembering that the Lord is a light that dwells within every man and woman equally. These are the sacred, merciful teachings of Grace, called the *Sat* Teachings.

In the Footsteps of the Masters

*Aim to devote your life entirely to work for God
and the benefit of all.*

An important key to remember is that all of the saints and masters want you to study their lives, live like them and walk in their footsteps. It is why Jesus the Christ said, *"Follow me"* (Matthew 4:19). The external garb does not matter much, for it is an inward change of the heart that matters. We change the heart by purifying it, through calling on the name of the Lord many, many times a day. If we are patient and have perseverance, we overcome the old ego and become a new divine being, abiding in the Beloved forever. The journey begins when you call out to Him and commit yourself to a new way of living in harmony with the universe, your brothers and sisters, and all of humanity, pledging to follow through on the guidance provided for you by the masters, the scriptures, and your guide-teacher.

The key to doing this is to be inwardly humble, open and trusting like a child, yet vigilant and discerning as you practice loving and serving others as yourself. By living in the footsteps of the masters, we develop Christ Consciousness, sharing pure, selfless love with every person, no matter what their creed, nationality, ethnicity or culture. Let this unbounded love flow forth from you and through you, living it now. Be it now for all humanity. Live a life of service by feeding the poor, clothing the naked, housing the homeless, healing the sick, and visiting people in prison. These are the things that Christ said we should do.

Aim to devote your life completely to working for God and the benefit of all. Let "service not self" be your motto. This is the true path, whereas when you work only for yourself, you remain incomplete and unfulfilled. Do all that you do for God and for others,
and in this way you can know your Self, and know that you are a part of God.

Do not let the seriousness of the world overcome you, stay as happy as you can, and do not worry. Let God be the focus of your love, rather than material things or money. See Him, sense Him, and intuit Him in everyone.

Whenever you think of Him, think of His Glory. It is all around you, everywhere, and it is within you, shining as your real Self. The way to that real Self is through humility and by seeking to serve instead of to be served.

I invite you to speak and sing God's words in the sacred texts and scriptures as your own, immersing yourself and becoming one with the living Presence in each word. Walk the walk and dance the dance of the divine life of the saints with joy. Give your life as an offering of love to God daily, keeping the feeling of God's love and bliss as the center point of your life.

The Name

The greatest spiritual practice in this age is to call on the name of the Lord.

Pray to Him without ceasing, call to Him without ceasing, and gradually you will abide in Him and He in you. You and He shall be one. This oneness is the goal of all paths and religions. Then you will realize that all names are His names.

The name is the root of every virtue and noble quality; it is the source of all love and oneness. I namaste and bow to the name of God within you and to the silence within you, both of which are the real, divine you. The way into the Kingdom of God within you is through the doorway of stillness and silent purity created by your constant repetition of the name. You can choose any name of God that feels comfortable and right to you in your heart, according to your faith.

Meditate on the following words: The name and the named are the same, God is non-different than His name. Speak the name of God with sweet words of love. The key is to say it with feeling, concentration and reverence as if you are calling out to God with your last breath.

Calling on the name of God will gradually cleanse your heart, clear your mind and awaken your divine consciousness so that you can merge into the vibrational harmony of the universe. It slowly removes all difficulties, darkness, selfishness, and sense of the lonely, separate self, called "me," "I," and "myself." The name sanctifies you, and purifies your heart into love and oneness. Remember: *"Whosoever shall call upon the name of the Lord shall be saved."* -Romans 10:13

As you say the Name with every breath, visualize cultivating love in your heart like you are growing a lotus of love and beauty that has the divine fragrance of God's bliss. Imagine you are sending that love forth to touch and heal the world.

Ceaselessly call His name, talk with Him and listen to Him throughout the day. The more that you call on the name of the Lord, the purer you will become, and the purer you become, the more you will become the name of God. Since God is His name, the more you become the name of God, the more you become God. Awaken.

No matter what you are doing at home or work, give your Beloved your whole heart. Love and adore Him, worship Him always, bow to Him only and you will find Him. This I promise you.

Our ultimate goal is to have our attention fixed on the Lord one hundred percent of the time. For example, when you are doing laundry, you can chant the name of God. Some chant the *Maha Mantra* from the *Bhagavad Gita*:

"Hare Krishna, Hare Krishna, Krishna Krishna, Hare Hare; Hare Rama, Hare Rama, Rama Rama, Hare Hare".

Or from *The Bible*,
"Lord Jesus Christ Have Mercy on Me!"

Commit the time that you are folding each article of clothing to chanting God's name. That way, the name of God goes into each piece, and you wear your clothing as a shield. When you are preparing food, you can chant as you cook your food. Give all of your food to God and imbue it with the name of God so that when you eat it, you take in that vibration (God) just as you would when receiving Holy Communion. While you shower, bathe or wash your face, you can make your body temple sacred by saying the name of God.

Call Him, and He will call you...all the way home. Call on the name of the Lord and He will set you free. Be patient, O lover of God, and never give up or give in, no matter what. When you call on the name of the Lord, your Supreme Beloved Lord who is All-Existence, All-Knowledge, and All-Bliss will manifest to you. All of the difficulties, forgetting God, and darkness will go away.

Begin this now. Remember to call His name a thousand times a day or more, and it is guaranteed that you will live with God forever. This is an experience in which your soul flies home to its real abiding place on wings of the name of God, as you also bless the Name and bless the Lord.

Your Real Self

*The goal is for you to awaken and be who you truly already are:
a soul who is a very real part of God,
the supreme fulfilling Love.*

The highest truth possible in this world is knowledge of the real Self. Your soul is the true lamp of knowledge itself, it is the only real You that you will ever truly know. This knowledge is far beyond the intellectual knowledge of the mind, it is deeper than all other forms of knowledge. True knowing is felt and can only be lived. In this way it is made real and realized.

*I namaste to your true Self, who dwells deeper than the mind, ego,
intellect, and remarkable performance-art that is your life.*

In India, the Self is described as *Sat Chit Ananda*, which is Sanskrit for truth, consciousness, and bliss. *Sat* means the highest truth, that you exist. *Chit* means that you are conscious. *Ananda* means you are blissful. You and God are both made up of these same three qualities. The only difference is in quantity. God is cosmically bigger and more infinite. Qualitatively you are the same as He.

God is embodied inside of you as a part of you. To be "a part of" means to be connected within a whole and complete union of oneness. This is your relationship with God, it is a relationship of non-separation. This means that God is always right where you are, with you, in you, as a part of you now at this exact moment. He created this life out of His love for you so that you could rediscover that there is a Divine Intelligence that does care about you. This Divine Intelligence is Love itself. You are the peace and lasting happiness that you are seeking…you are already Love right now.

To realize who you are, you must want the truth like a starving person wants food…it is that simple. Truth is One; we are One. The mind is a computer and to understand what I am saying is beyond its computational power. It cannot compute the loving experience that is the truth of who you are, which is Bliss itself.

Who you thought you were before this moment was an illusion, for who you really are is Love incarnate.

The "I", or the ego, is merely an accumulation of ideas about yourself given to you by your parents so that you could survive and get along. It is a cluster of thoughts based on self-centeredness, selfishness and constantly feeling in need. You are peace itself. You were hypnotized by the illusion of social conditioning, education and advertising into thinking that you were an incomplete, contracted ego that was lacking and needing something from outside itself to be complete. You desire to be happy because you want to be yourself. However, you have not been being yourself, you have been being what others have wanted you to be. Your mind causes you to identify with complexities, questions, problems and dramas. You cannot find the truth through the mind, for again I say, you are the reality of bliss.

What your soul is longing for is to feel the joyful fulfillment that is felt when you know that God dwells within you and everyone equally and that your self can never be separate from this perfect, blissfully loving Divine Being.

Once the soul discovers that chasing material desires and trying to fulfill them does not ultimately work, it begins to search (at first outside of itself) for "The Answer." Thus begins the process of awakening out of the hypnotized state by gradually turning one's focus inward. It is a journey of consciousness in which the false ego-identification dissolves in degrees by love into the heart-core of calm, peace and kindness that is your real Self.

There is only one thing that can 'woo' you away from the battles and distractions of this world; one thing that can entice you away from your desires that clamor like restless children…and that is God's love. Only God can entirely satisfy the deep hunger and yearning inside you. Desire infinite love more than anything in this world! Thus, you shall overcome the might of *Maya*, which is the power of illusion in this world that gives you the sense of separateness from others.

God is an experience of Love beyond the mind.

Wake up now! Consciously become aware of who you already are. Remember, if you want it enough, you shall become it. It is up to you. It is all about changing what you want in the deepest part of your heart, and wanting it so much that you are willing to change your life, put aside your ego and start over in the here and now. God will then lift you up by the grace that comes through the masters and a genuine teacher.

Each time one humbles oneself and the "I" opens, trusts and surrenders, existence is seen for what it is: an illusion dissolving into the only thing that is real — God. The Tibetans call it the death and rebirth of the ego out of misery and unhappiness into the unchained expansiveness of deep, spiritual, peaceful, loving, blissful Self-realization.

Once one knows who he or she really is—part of the Beloved—then, knowing the real Self, one no longer plays in the sandbox of ignorance. Instead, he or she enjoys God-consciousness, which is unrestricted love, freedom, wisdom, and bliss. The transformation to this state is who we already, always were in complete honesty, forever in this blissful new life in the Infinite.

Spiritual Practice

*Be true to your spiritual goal,
be true to yourself and have faith in yourself.*

The purpose of your life is to find God. Believe in and cultivate faith that you will ultimately succeed in life. Then know that it is single-minded, concentrated effort that guarantees your success. This requires devotion, which is the most essential quality that enables success to happen. Develop your devotion and channel it into a self-disciplined effort that is tenacious, concentrated, consistent and persevering. In all of your actions be patient, have forbearance, and always treat others the way that you would want to be treated, for whatever you put out will come back to you.

Remember that it is in giving that we receive. Your life is simply a reflection of what you have given to others in the past and in past lives. In this way you are the creator of either your success or failure. With each thought, word, and action you "cast your bread upon the water," and it returns to you. Wisdom, strength, harmony, and excellence are the result of living a life in which you love and treat others the way that you would like to be treated.

True knowledge teaches you that you should love others as yourself. It is born out of the sacrifices you are willing to make in your service to others. Love is born out of sacrifice. Your happiness is then born out of that love, and it is a lasting love and thus a lasting happiness. The path to lasting happiness is only found in the heart, not in the mind. That is why lasting happiness is only found in your heart, for your heart is the dwelling place of the Blessed Lord, your true Beloved.

Plant Him like a beautiful lotus in your heart. If you believe He is way up high above you and not in your heart, then that is called intellectual study, and it leaves you feeling left out of the real life that is possible for you. Take Him into your heart and plant Him there and then with your love, cultivate and grow your devotion, dedication, and practice. Develop an earnest and persistent daily practice that never gives up. You will find that God is all in all. He is one with everyone, including you.

Your soul can be imagined as a lotus, growing and pushing its way upward through the soil. It is your soul pushing upward against the hard ground that makes it strong. To become strong is half of the soul's purpose for coming to life on this planet. The other half of the soul's purpose is to express love by putting service before self. All of the strength and all of the power that you need is right inside you...believe it, believe in yourself. Self-will is important, yet give all that you do to God, asking that His will be done. Then His grace is upon you and you find the eternal, the place unchanging, liberation in Him. He is dearer than anything in this material world.

Accept everything as happening to you for a reason; often it is to teach a lesson. Learn the lesson while also remaining positive, and you will see that you are becoming stronger and stronger. It may not appear as so, but everything that happens has a lesson that accompanies it. The purpose of life is to gain an understanding of this truth, and also to discover the treasure that is within you, the "Pearl of Great Price", God as your love.

All the masters are very clear in stating the importance of having a daily practice. No matter how little or much it is, it is important to do it with the desire for God in mind. Remember why you are doing it and why you are reading this, which is to know God. Aim to change your life by making small lifestyle changes every day. As you persist, you will have Him, and having Him fulfills the entire reason for being on earth. This is the only reason why He comes to Earth or speaks through another. It is to make sure you and others surely make it home to Him, home to God.

Slowly increase the time each day that you give to your soulful study, while also going deeper and deeper into your chanting and meditation until you reach the state of bliss, ecstasy and peace which is there waiting for you now. It is worth the daily hard work and effort that you put into it. Who you really are is always self-evident if you will spend enough time developing loving awareness of God.

Stand ready and desirous of the true experience of the open heart in which you "awaken and remember" your love for your blessed Father-Mother God who is always dwelling within your heart. Begin anew now, for each new moment is a new beginning.

Finding The Beloved in All

*God resides in the heart of all beings.
Give Him your whole heart with the deepest, loving adoration.*

Behold, the true path of Love stands before you always...look and see, here it is. No matter what appears to be before you, around you, above you, or below you, in reality, O lover of God, this is all God — this is all your Beloved!

You can know Him here and now inside your heart, consciousness, and self. Pause now, and worship God in loving adoration. He is eternally with you, as well as all around you in every friend as every friend, and in every creature as every creature.

Aim to remember daily in your heart that you are the lover and God is your Beloved. When you also remember that your Beloved dwells in the heart of every being then you can gradually learn to love your Beloved in everyone, learning to love them as you would like to be loved as if you were them.

Listen, the more you love your Beloved who is everywhere, the more He gives that love back to you multiplied. He unveils your consciousness and removes the clouds from you enabling the Light to shine into your heart which makes you gradually happier and happier.

Simply begin to love more and more, making your daily meditation to love your children, your family, people, places and things while remembering in your heart that it is really all your Beloved. Then you will receive the great prize and golden goal of all life: a lasting love that never ends.

Practice loving the Creator, your Beloved, who is in every child, every flower, and everyone. Practice loving the Divine Ground of Love, which is within all, here and now. He is eternally with you, as well as all around you, dwelling within everything.

A Prayer to The Beloved:

I pray to the Supreme God,
The Highest of the high,
Creator of all universes, planes and dimensions:
To You alone, I bow and give my whole heart,
I love and adore You.
I surrender my all, my will, my actions
As I immerse constantly, daily,
In the warm bath of Your Love.
O, all-pervasive One
Who I feel here with me, always,
You art the sole indweller in every heart!

Thou art Divine Love in the lotus of everyone.
Thou art the undifferentiated God of Love.
Remind us constantly by day and night
To keep our minds on Thee;
To pray and call to you, chanting and calling out
Thy Name from our hearts.

Devotional Service

Let all your actions be done for the Lord with love.

To serve God is commonly understood, but to make Him happy is the expression of a true lover of the Beloved Lord. When you open, trust, surrender and dedicate yourself entirely to your greatest Love, the Lord, then you naturally want to serve Him and desire to make Him happy.

Live your whole life for love and service for God as the dearest of the dear and the nearest of the near. Remember to thank Him every day for your life, and bless Him, for He will always bless you back. Most importantly, tell Him you love Him from your heart. Of all things, this makes Him the happiest.

Daily, hourly, meditate on how you can make God happy, for that is the highest service you can do. The key to this true, loving relationship with God is to love Him in such a deep, wholehearted and complete manner that you have no desire for anything in return—not even peace, love or bliss necessarily. The joy of your love and service for Him becomes its own reward, it is pure, unselfish giving without wanting anything in return.

As you give your love to God every day, let your love for Him in everyone be your guide. Ask God during the day:

"Beloved, what would you like me to do? Show me what Your will is this day. Thy will be done in my life. I only wish to do Your will."

Give Him your life, your "kingdom" and say to Him:

"Father, I give you my kingdom. Let Thy kingdom come into my life."

Then give your will to Him and say,

"Father, I give you my will. Instead of my will, let Your will be done".

These are the first words of the *Lord's Prayer* which you can say periodically throughout the day and night, surrendering more and more of your life to Him. Surrender to Him first thing each day, and ask Him for ideas on how to solve your problems. Keep asking and keep your eyes and ears open, for if they are, you will see that He will give you a way forward.

Devotion is simply committed love. When you are devout, you have a loving commitment in your heart to stay the course, and run the good race all the way to the finish. Your love becomes so strong that you will persevere through all the storms and tests that will come.

Being fully devoted to the Lord means having one's mind fully fixed on Him at all times. We can measure our devotion by noticing just how much of the time we have the focus of our consciousness "knitted" in God. Aim to gradually train yourself to increase the amount of time that you keep your mind fixed on your Beloved Lord amidst your duties. Keep your mind fixed on God "on the back burner" while you do your work in the world with excellence "on the front burner."

Whatever you do, do it only for God, including all you are doing at this moment for Him. Whether you are reading a book, washing the dishes, taking care of your family, or driving a car, let all of your work be done to make the Lord happy and to satisfy Him with your love. Serve your friends, your family, your community, your country, the whole planet, only for God.

As Christ said, *"A new commandment I give to you, that you love one another"* (John 13:34). God is Love, and thus God alone is real. God is, God was, and God will always be…and you are part of that source of all Love. God loves Love, and only the attitude of devotion pleases Him. There is nothing else in all of creation that does so… only Love.

The Awakening of Divine Love

Let God glorify your life with His love, for His love on this earth manifests as the universal avatar of every age.

Every time you allow God's Divine Love to come through you, abandoning your selfishness then that is the return of the Christ, the universal avatar. God is calling everyone to enter into Divine Love and to let go of the veil of ignorance called selfishness. This great truth is the basic theme that runs through all religions and philosophies.

It takes hundreds of years, sometimes thousands, for people to recognize the avatar manifesting as Divine Love. The manifestation of Divine Love is the One Teacher expressing Himself through Jesus, Yogananda, Babaji, Ramakrishna, Meher Baba, Sathya Sai Baba, Neem Karoli Baba, and many more. Each master and teacher is a finger on God's hands, and He has many fingers everywhere in the world, from Delhi to Geneva to New York to Rio de Janeiro to Beijing.

Each avatar that comes to the earth always teaches a different expression of the same one God. Zoroaster manifested love as purity, Ram manifested love as truth, Krishna manifested love as playfulness, Jesus manifested self-sacrificing love, and Mohammed manifested zeal and fire for the love of God.

Divine Love is awakening the world and it is the same one Master who is behind all of it, as He transforms and awakens people out of the intellect. This is the greatest avataric expression that has ever occurred. It is beyond one individual, yet it is every teacher and every master, for it is for all of humanity on this planet and throughout the universe. This is the grand summation of the work of all the avatars of all previous divine manifestations. It is the return of the universal God of Love as Divine Love. Watch as it awakens those who are ready. Worship this divine love and accept it as the glory of God, the avatar on this Earth.

In reality, humankind has already been saved several times by the intervention of Divine Love. Krishna states in *The Bhagavad Gita* (Ch. 4:7-8) that whenever humanity gets lost, He will return to straighten things out for them by re-establishing love and right action.

He has returned through the masters, who have come from the East. Christ prophesied that the Christ will come out of the East with power and glory when he said, *"Just as lightning comes from the east and flashes as far as the west, so will be the coming of the Son of Man."* (Matthew 24:27)

He has come not as one person, but as one consciousness, the Christ Consciousness, the consciousness of a mother's and father's love, only amplified into God's Divine Love.

This same Divine Love is talking to you through these words and in essence it is you. Who you are is divine, perfect and one with the spirit of the avatar, the Christ, the Messiah, Love. It is the innermost nature, for everyone is the same inside, and no one is less than anyone else. In truth we are all one Being, as different fingers on the same hand of God, which is the universe, the cosmos.

I invite you to give yourself to this Divine Love completely like a little child. Open to it, trust it, and completely surrender to it. As you surrender, your conscious awareness expands into an experience of cosmic love. Thus you realize that the universe is your greater identity, and every part of yourself that you surrender to God in this process becomes pure, ecstatic bliss.

Your consciousness of yourself as the cosmos everywhere all around you and within you is the true reality. It is only the degrees of recognition and realization of this truth that makes it seem as though people are on different levels of development. In reality we are all equal beings, and the universe is our cosmic playground as our All-One-Self. Our Self and God are the same, appearing all around us right now as everyone and everything in our lives.

Come home to the loving form and glorious effulgence of the Lord, which is the boundless, ecstatic, blissful, indescribable intoxication of God-Conscious, perfect, fulfilling Love. This perfect Love is here, now, everywhere through every cell in your body and throughout your consciousness, heart, soul, mind and being. Thou Art Attainment Itself.

The following is a channeled message from the Christ. Please read each word slowly and take it in as a sacred and direct message to you now:

"My children,
I Am come that you may have life and have it more abundantly. Open now your hearts and receive Me, for I Am waiting to come forth in each of you consciously, so that you may not only know Me but that you may know that I Am your Self, your one and only Self.

The time has come that all may know Me if they will. Receive Me, O My children. Look for Me, not in some far-off time or place, but realize that I Am here and now in your hearts. I Am that love that is pushing forth to love you, bless you, and supply you with all good things needed for My harmonious and perfect expression through you.

Open wide your hearts, acknowledge and look to Me there constantly. Ever keep your ears turned to Me, listening for My voice, waiting thus upon Me in your heart as you go about your tasks or wish to know My will.

Take the time now to slow down and listen to your heart, for I promise I will not let any go unfed, unhealed, unsatisfied, whose hearts are fixed on Me. Even as you receive all of your life, health and strength from My life in you, so can you receive the fullness of My Life not only as perfect health and strength, but as perfect care, perfect supply, and perfect expression of My perfect nature — when you yield your mind and self over wholly to Me.

I receive you, and I bless you, My dear one. My love ever surrounds you and will always go before you, lighting your way and making easy your tasks if you will but trust Me and let Me lead and guide you in all your ways."

Remember

God is the Divine Ground of Being everywhere,
the All in all.

God is the love you feel for your children
and one another.

Love is the inmost self in every person, including
you.

Follow through on the guidance your teacher gives
you with an eternal, unwavering commitment.

The way to your real Self is through humility and by
seeking to serve instead of to be served.

Serve God in everyone.

Call on the Name of the Lord a thousand times a day.

Cherish the scriptures as love letters to you
from your Beloved Lord.

God is unlimited Truth, Consciousness, and Bliss,
and you are a tiny yet precious ray of His Being.

Do all that you do for God and others,
for this is the way that you can know your Self

and know that you are a part of God.
Let your ego be a zero, and you will be a hero.

God is an experience of love beyond the mind.

God is something you feel and know with absolute
certainty — that you are one with God here and now.

Love Him with all your heart and being
and love your neighbor as yourself.

Live a moral and courageous life as you do your duty.

Tell the truth.

Do not say anything if it does not add to the silence.

Self-effort and strength leads to a life lived more
abundantly.

Love everyone.

Forgive each other and be here now with each other.

Learn to love those you do not yet love.
Expanding your ability to love others opens your
heart.

Let the sunshine of your love
be your daily gift to the world,
for your love is proof of the existence of God.
God is the One that we live and move
and have our being in, for He is all existence.

Do all that you are doing in service for the Lord from
this moment on and to do it with love.

All this is God
and you are a part of Him here and now.

Thank God always for all you receive.
Bless Him, and He will always bless you back,
multiplied, and tell Him you love Him.

May you never forget God even for a moment.

Poetry

Welcome to Your Heart

This is where you reside.
Slow down now and listen…
You are safe and protected.
You dwell in the center of a luminous, divine, lotus
under the shelter of the Most High.

You are a child of the living God forever.
Through your love, you ascend…
On the wings of service, you fly
into the one solar body of radiant light.

This is the very center of your being,
The point from which the fire emanates
and the stars shine all around you.

You are a blazing sun – son of God,
you always were and always will be…
flying in love and service to all.

Child of My Heart

Behold in the sky:
The rainbow with its legend old,
the mythical story of the pot of gold,
appears often in the cloudy sky—
ye look and thrill and wonder why?

Consider well the clouds effect,
the background of the air so wet,
that iridescent jets of mist shine forth in colors rare,
revealing to all just this:

Lo, I Am Everywhere
and I Love You.

Above, below, within, without,
of this, there is no doubt.
The Holy One, Pure Spirit Light,
reveals to thee in earthly sight,
faint glimpses of Myself so free,
so in thy heart rejoice in Me.

I Am Beauty
and You are Me.

Beloved:
My holy church is the Universe.
I come to point in thee, thy life
through all eternity.

For you to understand and use Me
for a church, the earth the floor must be;
the horizon for the walls so tall,
the sky for roof upon the walls,
the sun, the heat, the light,
the stars, the candles at night,
the moon whose magic mystery
projects its incense over thee,
and all the glory of day and night I give thee
for thy delight.

The Holy Breath I breathe in thee.
Rejoice, receive, be free, be free.

I AM within thee.
Thou art Me.

The Warm Bath of God's Love

Relax into the warm bath of God's Love.
The Self is Love,
calm, centered and unmoving.
It shines out of the radiant, One Consciousness
within you and everyone equally.
Relax into the the all-pervasive, vast expansion
of Being that thou Art.

Behind this game of hide-and-seek,
we all are One…
dissolving into this perfect, warm ocean of God's
Love and Bliss that is all around us and within us —
AWAKEN.

Take a moment to feel the reality
of God's Omnipresence embracing you,
all around you like a warm blanket.
Lean back into this warm, loving embrace.
Feel the Love that is there.

Never give up, try more and more each and every
day.
It is all just a matter of tuning your feelings to the
Love.
First, you will sense a busy mind.

As you go deeper, you will sense a quieting of the mind,
and then emptiness.
With acceptance, this emptiness turns into peace.
At first, you may not recognize it,
but this peace is actually the very beginning of God's Presence.
Then, through practicing devotional service
for God and others, you will feel the Love.
The Love is the beginning of the nexus of God's Being;
the beginning of His innermost Nature;
the Truth that He Is.

There is nothing more fulfilling or wonderful
for you to experience in this life.
It is worth all the effort,
go for it every day.

Fix Your Mind on Him Always

Fix your mind on Him always;
do not let yourself be distracted.
Say His name from your heart with love,
and hold His light, glory, and image in your mind.

Prostrate at His feet, at the feet of His glory,
His Presence, and His image.
Now it is not seen as separate from yourself,
for it is part of you, and you are part of Him.
You both are one in the same;
one in this beautiful, fragrant Love.

This same fragrant Love
hides behind the multiplicity of forms called *maya*.
Maya is simply God's clothing that She
dresses and covers Herself with as Divine Mother
so that She can love and care for Her little children.

By learning how to meditate and call on the
name of God, the child now sees
behind all this temporary illusion of multiplicity,
that God is the One in all; He is One without a
second.

God is the one lasting happiness and fulfillment
that you can have now
by focusing on Him with Love.

Surrender to Him all that you are doing;
offer all of yourself to Him
in complete surrender.

Lay down all your work and your duties.
Love Him with all your heart,
love Him with all your soul,
love Him with all your strength,
love Him with all your mind,
love Him with all your self,
and give to Him all that you have.

Give it all to His work on the Earth
and say, *"Let Thy will be done!"*
Surrender...and let it all go,
putting yourself in His hands.

In Reality This is All an Ocean of Love

In reality this is all an Ocean of Love,
and reality is right here, right now.

This Ocean of Love
is fully conscious of you
and everything you do, everywhere you go
and everything you think you know.

What you think you know is simply built on models
that you were taught years ago
by people who just did not know anything about
the Divine Reality of Love
that is everywhere,
and its manifestation,
who is the *Sat* teacher.

It is your model of what a teacher is
that is keeping you from seeing the reality
of the s*at* teacher, who is
Total Love.
And he loves you totally
just for who you are,
not because he wants anything from you.

He just sees inside you
the Ocean of Divine Love
that you really Are…
For you and the s*at* teacher are one Divine Love,
God, the s*at* teacher, and the Self are One.

What is the "difference" between you and him?
He has only a thin veil of a personality,
just enough of an ego so that he can maintain a body.
He lives right here
on the edge of this void,
just watching and waiting
for you to have enough faith
to overcome your old ideas and models
so you can open, trust, and surrender completely-
reducing the veil of your ego down
enough so you can feel the genuine, authentic Love
for you that sees and loves you completely
for who you really are.

So be open, trust, and surrender your game;
have faith and surrender your ego.
Awaken and realize
your Self
by letting go and offering all that you do to the
Omnipresent, Oceanic Presence of Divine, Perfect
Love that is all around you…

Lay down all your duties into It
and surrendering into It;
Into the Love.

Your faith and complete surrender
activates the love,
which is Grace.
Grace is love in the form of the energy
that liberates
by dissolving the veil between you
and the Ocean of Love called God,
now.

See this Beloved Lord,
Original Creator of this creation,
the One God of the scriptures
as the One you have fallen in love with.
As whom you trust with your life absolutely.
As your real refuge and home
that you now melt and blend into.

One within the Consciousness of Bliss,
you are victorious over all problems,
and you shall now dwell in the highest
and most vast peace
that is beyond this changing world.
Dwell now in the eternal, divine state
of your pure, loving Being;

the Truth, Reality and the eternal Consciousness of Bliss.

The Lord says:
*"Surrender to Who I Am only,
to the One, eternal, ever-present Lord of Love,
with all of your heart's love
in committed, unwavering devotion.
Then you will know the truth
of My Supreme Love for you.
This is My sacred covenant with you."*

Give God all your life's work
with all its duties and obligations
letting go now of all fear.
You are hereby saved and delivered into this state of God's loving presence, surrounding you now.

The all-pervading Love
penetrates every cell and atom inside you.
This is your eternal, real, original home and refuge
in which you shall dwell with God,
happy forever more.

Namaste

Made in the USA
Columbia, SC
29 November 2018